God bless you,

[signature]

2019

Wrappings

Prayers, Poems and Reflections
BY PAULYNE CASCANETTE

Wrappings: Prayers, Poems and Reflections

Copyright © 2013 by Paulyne Cascanette

Requests for information should be addressed to:
cascanette@ibelievenetwork.com

Published by:
I Believe Network,
www.ibelievenetwork.com

ISBN# 978-0-9876870-3-6

Introduction

For as far back as I can remember, I have loved the Lord, but it wasn't until later in life when I actually read the Bible. There was a lot I didn't understand and much of it confused me, but when I read it, God's Word left me inspired and in awe. I saw it as a diary, a link, a guidebook; it was like looking through a telescope right into God's heart. No one should ever be deterred from reading it because they don't understand it.

Many years ago the Lord put on my heart to write a poem for each book of the bible, both the Old and the New Testament. With much prayer, and spiritual guidance, I am pleased to present to you, 'Wrappings'. This book is used as an introduction to God's Word, the Holy Bible, in the form of poetry, meditation and prayer. I have wrapped each book of the Bible with a poem. It is meant to draw the reader to the Scriptures.

Please bear in mind, it is *not* meant to replace your bible. After all, what person keeps the wrapping and tosses the gift. No, Wrappings is meant to draw you to the gift and the gift to God.

May God stir in you the desire to receive and explore His great gift of the Holy Scriptures.

Paulyne Cascanette

Table of Contents

Part One
The Old Testament

Genesis

Praise the Lord!
Praise the Creator of heaven and earth!
Behold the depth of His wisdom,
The capacity of His faithfulness,
The magnitude of His love.
Praise the Almighty God, your Father,
The Maker of heaven and earth.

Consider the Creator's amazing work.
Ponder anew the wisdom behind creation,
The love that sealed its perfection
And the faithfulness that certified the price regardless of its high cost.
Acknowledge His power and righteous intervention.
Lift up the Lord your God in highest tribute.
May all that has breath honour Him throughout all generations.

Great are You O Lord and most worthy of all praise.
The Heavens declare Your glory,
The Earth displays Your awesome works,
And Your creation proclaims Your mighty acts.
Let creation praise Your Holy Name.
Let all that has breath worship You O God.
Both now and forevermore.

Exodus

Sing to the Lord your God
O beloved nation.
Your God has heard your cry.
Hallelujah!!!
He comes like a flash of lightning
With the roar of thunder.
Surely your deliverance has come.
Therefore I say to you,
Praise Him, O ye His people.

Indeed we celebrate our God.
We sing unto the Lord
For He has given us a new song.
Hallelujah!!!
A song of joy, a song of victory.
Unto Him, we lift up our hearts,
With our lips, we sing our praises,
With holy hands we worship our God.
Truly, our song will be heard throughout all generations.

Through Moses and Aaron
The Lord our God...the true God
Has worked His mighty power.
Hallelujah!!!
We will praise Him forevermore.
He has remembered His covenant,
The promises He made to our forefather Abraham.

The land of our enemy will be our inheritance
And indeed, Israel will be the blessing of all nations.

Day and night, we reflect on His goodness:
With the bread of angels, He fed us.
With living water, He quenched our thirst.
Hallelujah!!!
He was our shelter from the scorching sun
And the light through the darkness.
His protection was on all sides.
Truly, He is worthy of our praise and song.
For, Love and Faithfulness led us through.

Time after time, we tried His patience.
With grumbling and distrust, we grieved Him.
Yet, He did not give us over as we rightly deserved.
Hallelujah!!!
Love and Faithfulness stood firm.
Could such love and devotion exist???
Yea!
God Himself is the Author of such love.
His mercies will be made known from generation to generation.

Let the sound of our praise be heard always.
We praise God, who made us a peculiar nation,
Who made us more numerous than the stars in the sky.

Hallelujah!!!
Our enemies cringe before us.
They fear our God, who defends us,
And they, who do not, are fools.
Their destruction is an example
Of God's allegiance to His own.

To God be the glory
Forever and ever.
Amen.

Leviticus

Behold your God, O Israel!
Be holy for the Lord your God is holy.
He set His laws and decrees before you,
To make you a holy people,
A people set apart for Himself.

Write His statutes and commands in your heart.
Teach them to your children.
The Lord your God is holy.
He desires a holy people
Who will serve Him wholeheartedly.

Do not take the Lord your God for granted,
Nor belittle what He has done for you.
Do not push Him away, like a second thought.
Love Him with all your heart, mind and soul.
Offer Him the sacrifice of your lips.

The Lord your God is holy and righteous.
With fear and awe, serve Him.
You are a distinctive people,
Therefore be a holy and godly people
Careful to walk in all His ways.

Numbers

(An oracle)

God,
You are most awesome!
You are the God of order and excellence.
Your love is endless,
Your faithfulness, everlasting.
In wisdom and in might
You set your design in motion.
You are altogether perfect.

Israel,
You are most blessed!
Out of all nations,
God has chosen you to make Himself known.
God has chosen you, O Israel,
To be the mirror image of His bride,
To reflect His awesome love and faithfulness.
You are altogether unique.

Israel,
Although you were unfaithful,
God remained true.
Although you rejected Him,
He never abandoned you
And although you rebelled,
You flourished through His discipline.
He is altogether excellent.

Deuteronomy

Choices...
They bring blessings,
Or they bring curses.
They lead to life and prosperity,
Or to death and destruction.

God...
Is a God of love,
A God of reverence.
He is also a God of justice,
A God of chastisement.

Decisions...
Walk in truth and light,
And live.
Or walk in deception and darkness,
And die.

Choices...
Let love be your guide,
Wisdom, your path.
Let perfection be your goal,
And fear your deterrent from blasphemy.

Rejoice!
The God of Abraham, Isaac and Jacob,
Has made known the path of life
To you and to those yet to be born.
O praise the greatness of our God!

Joshua

We are marching to the Promised Land.
In the strength of the Lord, we are marching.
Not by our own strength
But by the power of God.
We lay claim to the land flowing with milk and honey.

Lift your voices
O ye nation of the Lord
Lift up your voices
And proclaim His great love
A love so vast and immeasurable.

We are marching in the Name of the Lord.
Fear grips our enemies.
Nations flee before us.
The hand of the Lord is powerful,
Who can come against Him?

Praise to God.
Praise to the Almighty and awesome God,
Faithful and true,
Powerful and mighty.
Praise be to God!

Judges

Let all who know the Almighty
And let all who love the Lord
And all that has breath
Rejoice with me,
For God is most excellent and glorious.
He excels in mercy and compassion.

In awe I stand amazed.
From a distance, I see a nation,
A nation that stands above all other,
A living revelation to the world,
A revelation of God's dreadful judgments,
A revelation of God's love and mercies.

I say, woe is me,
For you, Israel, have rejected your God
And are following after devils.
You have forsaken your first love
To follow after your own destructive ways.
Time after time you grieve the heart of God.

O perverse and unfaithful nation
When will your rebellion cease?
Open your eyes, O you His people.
Open your heart to your God.
Faithful is He, slow to anger,
Quick to forgive, quick to bless.

Awaken O God's most precious nation,

Awaken and acknowledge your God.
Remember His mighty deeds done on your behalf.
Declare His love and compassion.
Subscribe honour and glory to the God of your youth.
Repent from your wicked ways. Repent.

Ruth

How magnificent is our Redeemer!
He is a shelter and a refuge,
A safe haven to all who turn to Him.
His love surpasses any love known to man,
His compassion knows no boundary,
His kindness reaches beyond all expectancy.
His goodness is known
Throughout all generations.

How great is our Redeemer!
Great is He, who redeems from darkness,
He who transforms sorrow and affliction
Into joy unspeakable.
Blessed are they whose God is the Lord,
He helps them through their troubles.
A people yet to be born will exalt Him.
To God be the glory, now and forevermore.

1 Samuel

O, Saul, my heart grieves as I observe
How you, who came from the smallest tribe of Israel,
You, who were anointed by the Lord,
To be king over Israel,
Have been rejected by God Himself.
He has torn the kingdom from your hand
And given it to someone after His own heart.

Saul, like a madman on a mission
You pursued David throughout the country and desert land.
You hounded him like a dog.
You hungered and thirsted for his destruction.
Jealousy drove you to insanity.
Hatred blinded you from the truth.
O Saul, your wicked heart was your greatest enemy, not David.

The Lord looks at the heart.
He desires obedience over sacrifice.
A pure and contrite heart, He delights in.
Saul, had you been faithful unto the Lord,
He would have established your kingdom over Israel forever.
But God has found disobedience and rebellion within you.
Arrogance crowned your soul.

Your guilt, O Saul, was not hidden.
Your stubborn and unrepentant heart
Grieved the Lord your God.
Can fresh water and salt water flow from the same spring?
Can a fig tree bear olives?
Neither can God tolerate sin.
Alas, you have lost your Crown of Glory!

2 Samuel

Behold the God of Israel,

The Omnipotent and All-Powerful God.

His power is displayed in all the Earth.

Be still

And observe the power of God:

He accomplishes great and awesome wonders.

He drives out nations along with their gods.

At His rebuke, He wipes out a whole people.

He alone is God; He alone is to be feared.

He gives strength and power to His anointed

And gives him victory over his enemies.

O my soul, perceive the power of God and acknowledge His wisdom.

Who can discern the wisdom of God?

Who can grasp its full measure?

His wisdom masters the universe.

Be still

And observe the wisdom of God:

Man's heart is not so profound that God cannot decipher it.

His soul, not too complex for Him to comprehend.

When sin and injustice abound

The Lord administers discipline and correction.

Blessed is he who practices justice

For he shares in God's wisdom.

O my soul, grasp the wisdom of God and cherish His love.

Can God's love be measured?

Can its boundaries be set?

His love embraces the universe.

Stand in awe,

And observe the love of God:

Though we deserve damnation,

His love redeems.

Though we fail,

His love is patient.

Though we grieve him,

His love is gracious.

O my soul, embrace the love of God, and worship the Almighty.

The Lord is Omniscient

Worthy is He of all praise and adoration.

His sovereignty covers the universe.

Sing out

And exalt the Lord your God.

Rejoice in the King of kings,

He is the Everlasting, the Mighty God.

Sing praises unto Him,

He is your shield and strength.

Acclaim His awesome wonders,

He is your Salvation.

O my soul, worship the Lord and magnify the one and only true God!

1 Kings

Beware prophet of Baal!
Your prophecies derive from lying spirits.
You speak to satisfy wicked ears,
And use deception for self-gain.
Beware O impostor,
For your punishment is at hand.

And you, O misguided prophet of God,
How gullible you are.
Although your heart was steadfast,
You have fallen prey to deception.
I say woe to you, O foolish prophet,
For you bring destruction upon yourself.

But you, O true prophet of God,
Blessed are you, for truly you are His voice,
His faithful messenger.
You serve Him consistently at any cost.
Therefore I say, blessed are you O faithful prophet
For the glory of God is your crown.

2 Kings

Is there greater fear to face,
Than God's burning anger?
Or anything worse
Than God's irrevocable rejection?

Who can shift God's heart?
Or alter His pronounced judgment?
Surely no one can bear God's wrath
Or withstand His consuming fire.

Who can divert His set mind?
Who can touch His heart,
And stifle His anger?
Does such a man exist?

He who fears the Lord,
Who serves with integrity and uprightness,
He who rules in truth and justice,
It is he, who moves God's heart.

1 Chronicles

Rejoice, O son of Jesse,
God is well aware of your heart's desire.
Although you are not the one to build His temple,
He will give you the details and understanding of His plans.
Your son Solomon is the one to build His house of prayer.
Your intentions please Him,
For He knows your heart
And the motive behind your thoughts.

O Lord, it pleased You
To bless David and his house forever.
Great are You O Lord
And faithful is Your Name,
For You stand true to Your word.

Beware, O son of Jesse.
The enemy is a roaring lion,
Seeking whom he may devour.
He will use your weakness of passion and pride
To crush your spirit and your loyalty to God.
He seeks to incite you to do evil,
Evil against yourself
And evil against the Lord your God.

O Lord,
Though You punish misdeeds,
You are quick to forgive
Quick to bless
For You stand true to Your people.

2 Chronicles

O king of Judah,
God established you as king
To maintain justice and righteousness.

Blessed are you
O faithful kings of Judah,
For you glorify the Lord your God.
You govern with the scepter of the King of kings,
And take up the cause of the people.
Blessed are you, O loyal kings,
For you rule with fear and reverence.

But you, O unfaithful kings of Judah,
Cursed are you,
For you reject the Lord your God
And govern with the scepter of evil.
You exalt the wicked and trample the innocent.
Cursed are you, O corrupt kings,
For you rule in ignorance and foolishness.

O king of Judah,
God established you as king
To bring glory and honour to His Name.

With one mind and one heart
You built God a temple,
A place for sacrifice and worship.
What splendor, what magnificence!

Your temple O Lord
Radiates Your glory and beauty.
You delight in the heart, which built it.

Praise Him, O ye His people.
For His love endures forever.
Enter His gates.
Lift up your hearts and worship Him,
Offer sacrifices of a pure and contrite heart.
Praise Him, O you His kings,
For His love endures forever.

Ezra

The God of Israel has done marvelous things.
True to His word,
He has gathered His people from amongst the nations,
And returned Israel to their inheritance
That they may worship as a nation in His holy temple.

Praise be to the Lord our God,
Who extended the king's goodness to Israel,
And appointed us to rebuild God's temple,
That we may worship and honour Him.
Praise the Lord for His endless love and mercy.

Grief and remorse pierce my heart
As I remember the desolation our sin has caused
And to find the holy remnant
Mingling with the people around her,
A people corrupt with evil practices.

With a broken and contrite heart
We turn from our sin.
In tears we repent from our unfaithfulness.
We lift up our hearts and our voices
To worship You O Lord, O merciful God.

We worship God in His holy temple.
In the inner sanctuary of our hearts, we exalt Him,
For He is holy and righteous.
We lift Him up in praise and honour
For His love and mercy endure forever.

Nehemiah

Our hearts ached, for great was our tribulation.
As we set out to rebuild the city walls,
Our enemies tormented us day and night.
The more we worked
The more they mocked and ridiculed us.
When the gaps of the walls were being closed,
Their anger flared and they plotted to fight against Jerusalem.

Our hearts cried out, for great was our distress.
As one man, we sought the Almighty.
We mourned, fasted and called out to God in prayer.
Great is the Lord for He hears our cry.
He is quick to respond, quick to help.
He is our shelter and our strength.
Our burden is great, but greater is our God.

Worthy is our God, worthy of all praise.
He renews our strength and lifts our head.
In front of our enemies' eyes, we gained the victory.
Their wickedness has fallen on their own heads.
Great and mighty is the one and only true God, our God.
Be exalted O God, for You are worthy,
Worthy to receive the praise of Your people.

Esther

The Lord's blueprints are laid out.
His mission set in motion.

Nothing and no one can alter His plans.
He fulfills His purpose.

With divine intervention
He dissuades man's evil intents.

Blessed are they, who trust in Him
Who fight the good fight with Him.

His saints trample down their enemy
They are doomed from the beginning.

Just and merciful is the Almighty God,
Who rules with the scepter of love.

Job

My God, why does Your anger burn hard against me?

You have devastated my entire household.

My children, You have taken from me.

My wife finds me repulsive.

My frame is but a shadow.

You have stripped me of my honour.

My friends torment me with pumped up wisdom and knowledge.

My God, what have I done to deserve such calamity?

Though I am guiltless, You afflict me.

I am innocent, yet You deny me justice.

I, a righteous and blameless man, am reduced to a mere laughing stock.

My God, why do You rebuke me so severely?

Woe is me, for I have spoken out of ignorance

And without understanding.

Truly, I was a brute beast before You.

In ashes I repent, O Mighty God.

You are just and right in all You do.

Your purpose perfects me.

No one has the power to foil Your plans.

Praise God,

For my ears had heard of You

But now my eyes have seen You.

My heart knows no greater love.

Praise God, praise God!!!

Psalms

Psalms,
A solace, a sanctuary.
How I love to meet with Him
In the closet of His holy word,
In the very soul of scripture.

With the psalmist,
I delve in the meditations of the heart.
With a sacred song
I share inner thoughts
That come from deep within my very soul.

Intimate moments, precious moments,
Secrets, undisclosed matters,
All lay bare,
All in the open,
Expressed, revealed, shared.

Psalms,
The voice of one's heart
The prayer of a lowly soul
The tongue of praise
The declaration of a renewed spirit.

To God be the glory!
To Him who keeps not His distance from us
But draws us to Himself.
Yes, to Him be the glory both now and forevermore.
Amen!

Proverbs

Wise are they who fear the Lord.
Blessed are they who acknowledge God.
Great are they whose strength is the Almighty,
And wealthy are they whose treasure is God's word...
Theirs is the kingdom of God.

Dull are the minds that know not the Lord.
Sightless are the eyes that are blind to the Almighty.
Foolish are the hearts that love not God,
And damned are the feet that walk away from salvation...
Theirs is the kingdom of darkness.

There are two things that are most wise,
Three that are supreme:
They who walk in the ways of the Lord,
They who are God-fearing,
And they who acknowledge the Almighty God.

Ecclesiastes

Toil, achievement, success,
What does one gain by it all?
So much effort put into labour,
Only to hand it all over at the end of life.
Meaningless! All meaningless,
A chasing after the wind.
What is the profit of all this striving?
Is it not to find satisfaction in your toil?
To accept your lot and to be happy in your work?
For this is the gift of God.

Animals, fools, the wise,
Do they not all have the same end?
All strive to live and all die.
Meaningless! All meaningless. ￼
What does one gain by being wise?
Is anything under heaven said or done that is new?
Does wisdom promise length of days?
What then is the purpose of it all?
Won't both the wise and the fool come to judgment?
However, only one will stand upright before God.

There is a time and a season for all things.
A time to learn, a time to absorb.
A time to speak, a time to be silent.

We live, we die, and life goes on.
You ask, what is the purpose of it all?
Here then is the conclusion of the matter:
The whole duty of man
Is to glorify and honour the Almighty God,
To live for Him who gave His all,
To walk in His ways and make a difference.

Song of Songs

Your love is a priceless gift,
More precious than precious gems.
My love for you is a wrapping of gold
Tied with ribbons of silver.
Our love is looked upon with favor
Admired by all,
Desired by all.

I am faint with love.
Your awesome love fills my whole being.
It is a garden of wild flowers in full bloom.
Its beauty captivates my senses,
Its fragrance renders me breathless.
I bid you, O world,
Do not disturb love.

O love most magnificent!
Who can measure its depth?
Or fathom its power?
Your love knows no boundary
No power equals it.
Love's voice resonates in symphony
Rapturing my very soul in its melody.

Isaiah

Woe is me, I am undone!
How can I, a mere man stand before God?
I, in my sin-stained garment,
How can I stand before Love and Righteousness?
O Lord, I am speechless before You.
Cleanse me with the fire of Your love.

A vision unfolds before my eyes,
A vision of Israel, God's beloved nation.
My heart aches and is faint.
My spirit is devastated within me.
Woe, O Israel
For you have pierced God's heart.

Destruction and death cover the land.
A purifying fire sweeps across the nation.
Your wooden gods are reduced to ashes.
The nations you trust have forsaken you.
Your nakedness is exposed.
Where is your glory now, O Israel?

O Zion, precious are you to His heart.
He will redeem you with His own blood,
And the glory of the Lord will be revealed.
Amazing grace, amazing grace indeed!
Man has never known such devotion and compassion.
Come, O Israel, come worship the Lord your God.

Jeremiah

O my beloved, How you have grieved me!
Have I not been a husband to you, faithful and true?
Have I not loved you beyond measure?
Have I not provided for all your needs and more?
Have I not met all the requirements of a husband?

Then why, O my beloved, why have you forsaken me?
All I asked for was your love and your faithfulness.
Yet you could not give it.
Did I ask for so much? Was I so demanding?
Due love and respect, you denied me.

Time after time, I rescued you from affliction of your own making.
Time after time, I healed your wounds and nursed you back to health.
Yet, time after time you returned to folly.
You turned your back on the One who loved you most.
You pierced my heart.

You turned a deaf ear to my word and rejected me.
You have broken the terms of the covenant,
Therefore, I can no longer show compassion.
I will bring bereavement and destruction.
I, the Lord have decreed disaster for you.

Those you lusted after will ravage you.
Those to whom you exposed your nakedness, will shame you.
Those you trusted in will spew you out.
Your enemies will enslave you
And bring you to a strange land.

However, because I love you with an enduring love,
I will not totally annihilate you.
I will remember the covenant I made with your forefathers.
I will bring you back to your land
And once again I will be your God, and you, my people.

Lamentations

O daughter of Zion
Once cloaked in majesty
Now shrouded with God's anger,
Once called the perfection of beauty
Now the city of disgrace,
Woe to you for your punishment has come.

How my heart grieves
To see such splendor
Come to such ruin.
God's pride and joy
Has been crushed.
His anger is fired up.

Tell me, O virgin daughter of Judah,
Tell me, if you have strength left,
Why did you reject your God?
Why did you resort to such wickedness?
Your immorality could no longer be tolerated.
You have brought destruction upon yourself.

Zion, how you have fallen,
Fallen from such height.
Your song and dance
Has turned to mourning and lamentations.
Your children have been ravaged,
Your land raped.

But listen, Israel,
Your God is a faithful God.
He will not reject you forever.
His wrath will subside.
In your sorrow and repentance
He will return with compassion and love.

Ezekiel

Woe unto me,
I am undone.
With its every beat,
My heart aches,
My soul is weary,
My spirit is faint within me.
What have we done?

He is God,
The Sovereign Lord!

He loved us with an everlasting love,
Yet, we did not give Him our affection
But gave it to devils.
He was ever faithful
Yet, we didn't acknowledge Him.
We behaved as a harlot
And profaned His holy Name.

He is God,
The Holy One in Israel!

Woe,
Woe unto me,
I am undone.
Such grief and sorrow,
Such pain and insolence,
Such cruelty we have inflicted
Upon the Lord our God.

He is God,
The Lord Jehovah!

To God be the glory
Now and forevermore.
Worthy is He to receive,
All glory, honour and praise.
Let the world be filled with His renown,
For His love endures forever,
His faithfulness, for all eternity.

He is God,
The Omnipotent Yahweh!

Daniel

Behold the Almighty God:
His body is like chrysolite.
Ever present,
Ever faithful to His own.
A God of mystery,
A God of wonder.

His face is like lightning.
His eyes like torches,
Dispelling the deepest darkness.
A God of hope,
A God of security.

His eyes are like flaming torches.
He reaches the depths of our soul,
He sees all and knows all.
A God of justice
A God of mercy.

His arms and legs are like gleams of burnished bronze.
Arms that shield us,
Legs that walk through fire with us.
A God who comforts
A God who saves.

His voice is like the sound of a multitude.
He speaks and all creation stands still.
He speaks and it is done.
A God of authority,
A God of infinite power.

Behold the Almighty God:
His way is perfect,
His word flawless,
His wisdom awesome,
His love boundless.
Behold your God!

Hosea

I know not of love so vast
As the love God has for His people.
And I know not of faithfulness so deep
As the faithfulness He has shown His people.

They have torn His heart
As a ravenous beast tears its prey.
They have grieved Him to no end
And displayed nothing but contempt for Him.

They committed the vilest adultery against the Holy One,
And worshiped idols made with their own hands.
They lusted after nations that ridiculed them,
And acknowledged not God their Maker.

For a season His anger burned against them,
But with faithfulness only God could have
And a love mere man cannot fathom,
He had compassion and did not carry out His fierce anger.

Who is wise?
Let him acknowledge God's wondrous ways.
Who is discerning?
Let him understand.

Joel

The Lord, the One and only, is God.
His anger is upon Jerusalem.
His wrath covers your land, O Judah.
Who can endure?

The Lord, gracious and compassionate
Is slow to anger and abounding in love.
O beautiful Zion, render your heart unto Him,
And see His fury turn into blessing.

Rejoice O Zion, for the day of the Lord is at hand.
His Spirit will be on His people,
His sickle upon His enemies.
The Lord, He is God and there is none other.

Amos

O Israel, my people.
Is it not you that I have chosen,
Chosen out of all the nations of the world?
Have I not loved you with an everlasting love?
Yet you have rejected me.

Though I have blessed you beyond measure
You have turned from me.
You have been unfaithful
Your pride O Jacob, I abhor.
Your wicked ways disgust me.

You do not know how to do right.
I withheld my goodness from you,
And unleashed my anger upon you,
Still you would not return to me.
You refused to seek me and live.

Therefore I say, prepare to meet your God, O Israel.
Your enemy will drag you away
Away from your inheritance to a foreign land.
Though you were once a great multitude,
Only a remnant shall remain.

I will remember my covenant with David
And because I love you,
I will not utterly forsake you.
I will bring you back to the land I have given you
Never to uproot you again.

Obadiah

This is what the Lord says,
"Brothers are bonded through blood.
They protect and defend one another.
When your brother is in need,
Are you not to be first to help him?
Yet, you Esau,
Have turned on your own blood.
You rejoiced over his calamity.
You not only reveled in his trouble
But joined in the pillage.
O fool, your pride deceives you.
Your wicked schemes will fall on your own head.
Disaster will overtake you and destroy you.
Jacob, the Lord is faithful and true.
Though you have been trampled on,
You will not be utterly crushed.
You will have your inheritance."
The Lord has spoken.

Jonah

From darkness I called You,
And You heard me.
From the deep I cried out,
And You answered.
From the bottom of the pit,
You reached out to me and You rescued me.
When death overshadowed me,
You restored my life.

Your grace and compassion move me.
You, O Lord my God are amazing!
You are slow to anger,
And deter calamity.
What I considered dross,
You perceived as precious.
What I deemed worthless,
You reckoned valuable.

I sit here in awe as I consider my God.
Never have I known such love
Such compassion.
Surely man could never fully comprehend
The magnitude of the Lord's goodness.
Truly, our God is an awesome God.
Praise the Almighty God
O praise His Holy Name!!!

Micah

A vision...
Look, the Lord has awakened
As it were from a deep sleep.
The stench of sin permeates His nostrils.
The flames of His anger flare up
Unleashing the fury of His wrath.

Listen, the Lord comes
Riding on chariots of fire
Swooping throughout the land
Purging, purifying
The dross from amidst His people.

Behold, the Lord's excellence:
His mercy extinguishes His fiery anger,
His compassion halts warranted destruction.
Who can surpass our God
In forgiveness and pardon?

The Lord excels in beauty.
He comes robed in mercy,
Crowned in compassion.
Love is His name
And faithfulness His trait.

Nahum

God is a holy and righteous God.
Slow to anger yet intolerant of wickedness.
He is a jealous and avenging God.
Beware you evildoers,
God is against you.
Who can withstand His wrath?

God will annihilate the vile and the vicious.
He will bring to light their dark practices.
Shame will garb the harlot,
Destroyers will fall in their own traps,
Their evil schemes will revert back to them.
Cursed are you, you brood of vipers.

Praise the Lord, O saints of God.
Lift up your head, and take heart,
As a mighty warrior, He comes to save
He restores those who put their trust in Him.
He comes with healing and consolation.
He is a shield to those who call on His Name.

But you, O city of blood, tremble!
For you have tormented His people.
The Lord has set Himself against you.
Therefore prepare to meet your doom.
Because of your corruption and oppression
You will be completely destroyed!

Habakkuk

Who can discern the wisdom of God?
Or understand His ways?
Who can perceive the extent of His power?
Or fully grasp His love?

God is not blind to corruption and lawlessness,
Nor is He deaf to revelry and strife.
God is not unaware of man's distress,
Nor unresponsive to his cries.

The Omnipotent is faithful to act,
The Holy One, quick to resolve.
Awesome is the Lord the Almighty God.
His deeds and His eminence fill the earth.

Though arrows may pierce my heart
And darkness cast its shadows,
Yet, I will rejoice and be glad in the Lord.
In His strength I am renewed and refreshed.

Zephaniah

Woe to the complacent.
Woe to the degenerates of the land.
Woe to them who reject correction.
Woe! O Woe! Again, I say woe to you.
The great and dreadful day is quickly approaching,
The day of the Lord's fierce anger.

Blessed are the humble of the land
Who seek righteousness,
Who speak no lies and no deceit is found within.
The Lord, the One and Only, will care for them.
He will quiet them with His love.
He will restore their inheritance.

The Lord is merciful and just.
He bestows justice.
The wicked, He will bring to a sudden end,
And the righteous, He will re-establish.
His faithfulness is limitless,
His love infinite.

Haggai

Give careful thought my people,
Very careful thought to your ways.
You have built up your houses,
Yet my temple lies in ruins.
You have set priority on things of earth.
It is no wonder your blessings are so few.
With eyes wide open
Consider your poor behaviors.

Give careful thought
Of how, with such pride and joy
The day the foundation was laid.
O how your hearts burned within (Selah)
Oh my people,
How desolate destruction has left you.
Open your heart
To matters which hold eternal value.

Give careful thought to Me.
Open wide your arms
And receive the blessings I have for you.
Though you have fallen,
I will bless you
And remain with you,
Because I have chosen you,
Declares the Almighty God.

Zechariah

Tell me, what do you see?
I see the faithfulness of the Lord.
I see Him as it were, awakening from sleep.
His blessing is on the remnant of Israel.
He has determined to do good to Jerusalem and Judah.
The sound of laughter and rejoicing will be heard.
Once again, old men and women will sit on Jerusalem's streets,
And boys and girls will be playing there.

Tell me, what do you see?
I see the righteousness of the Lord.
I see His anger burning against Israel's enemies.
Woe to them who bruised the apple of His eye,
He renders powerless the powerful.
Woe to them who plundered His people.
His judgment is upon them.
The God of Israel is a jealous and consuming fire.

Tell me, what do you see?
I see the salvation of the Lord.
I see Him riding on a colt, gentle and righteous.
He comes proclaiming peace
And with the blood of His covenant, He sets the prisoners free.
Rejoice, O daughter of Zion,
Sing O daughter of Jerusalem,
Your King has come, live in truth and in peace.

Malachi

Priests of the Almighty God,
You question His love
You ask how you have shown contempt for His Name,
How you defiled Him,
How you wearied Him,
How you turned from Him.
Listen carefully, O you His messengers
For the Lord Himself will answer you...

I the Lord have blessed you.
I have chosen you above your brother.
Now I ask you this,
Where is the honour and respect due me?
Do you not show contempt at my table?
Do you not defile it by offering diseased and crippled animals?
Do you not weary me with your words?
Do you not turn from me when you turn from my decrees?
Do you not rob me in your tithes and offerings?

O, you His servants,
Serve Him with fear and reverence
Lest you be cursed,
For God is not blind
That He cannot see your heart,
God is not deaf
That He cannot hear your vulgarity
And God is not oblivious
That He cannot discern your insolence.

Part Two
The New Testament

Matthew

What man is this, this Jesus? ...
He is the King of kings,
Emmanuel, God with us,
The Christ, the Messiah,
The Son of David, the Son of man.
What man is this?
He is Jesus, God in the flesh!

What man is this, this Jesus? ...
He is the King of Israel,
The Master, the Righteous Servant,
The Living Word, the Great Physician,
The Good Shepherd, the Deliverer.
What man is this?
He is Jesus, God in action!

What man is this, this Jesus? ...
He is the King of the Jews,
The Passover Lamb, the Holy Sacrifice,
The Redeemer, the Liberator,
The Perfect Offering, the Savior.
What man is this?
He is Jesus, God of intercession!

What man is this, this Jesus? ...
He is the King of glory,
The Resurrection, the Everlasting Hope,
The fountain of living water, the Bread of life,
The Way, the Truth,

What man is this?
He is Jesus, God, the Great I Am!

What man is this, this Jesus? ...
He is the King Eternal,
The Alpha and the Omega,
The Beginning and the End,
The Supreme Ruler, the Lord of all.
What man is this?
He is Jesus, God the Omnipotent!

Jesus, Lord God almighty,
To you be all the glory
Both now and forevermore!

Mark

Jesus! God with us!
How lovely, how awesome,
Not with outer beauty
To attract us as the world does,
But Your piercing eyes,
Your captivating character,
Your heart, O, Your heart,
Who can withstand such magnificence?

Jesus, precious Lamb of God!
You flood our soul with life
And quicken our spirit,
You alone are precious and mighty.
You humble the high and lofty
And lift the lowly and broken.
Mighty and powerful are You
O precious Lamb of God!

Jesus, Living Sacrifice!
Perfect and complete,
Not a substitute, not a proxy,
But You Yourself, God in the flesh
Nailed to a rugged cross,
Demolished death's stronghold
And opened wide Heaven's gates.
Be Thou exalted, O most High God!

Luke

Hidden contemplations, hidden wonders
Stored deep in my heart throughout the years
Surface as I look upon my son,
A lamb torn apart by wild beasts,
Nailed to the old rugged cross,
A sword, a sword pierces my heart...

What man is this,
Who is conceived by a virgin?
Who shepherds worship and adore?
Who wise men seek?
Who kings fear?
Who astounds teachers of the law?

What man is this,
Who opens blind eyes?
Who unstops deaf ears?
Who stills the storm?
Who heals the sick and forgives sin?
Who raises the dead?

What man is this,
Who speaks with authority?
Who demons fear?
Who shuts the mouths of fools?
Who unveils things to come?
Who calls God 'Father'?

And what man is this,
Who concerns himself of others during his pain?
Who doesn't defend his innocence?
Who stands condemned and sets the guilty free?
Who prays for his killers?
What man is this???

O my son, my son...
O! MY GOD!!!!

John

Great is Your love O God!
It is wider than the heavens
Deeper than the ocean
Higher than the highest mountains.

O majestic love of God!
How beautifully expressed through Christ,
Not only spoken
But lived out to the fullest.

Amazing love!
Could it be revealed any better?
Surely not!
For even unto death, love reigned.

O love divine!
Pure and infinite love,
Christ has imparted a new vision,
He has made known the heart of God.

Acts

Together we work,
To bring light and life to a dying world,
Hope and deliverance to a broken world.
We, as Your messengers
And You, our Guiding Light.

In the name of love,
In Your mighty Name
We walk through thick and thin,
We tread the rugged road
And sail the stormy seas.

To the hungry,
We bring the Bread of Life.
To the thirsty,
We bring Living Water.
To the lost, we bring the Word of Life.

O, the love
That moves mountains!
The passion
That alters a set course!
O, the mighty power of God!
To God be the glory, honour and power
Both now and forevermore.

Romans

God's laws and principles reveal His character.
All that is beautiful and good is clear.
Love in its perfection is unfolded.
His righteous ways are made known to me,
O, how I yearn to walk in them.
Woe is me!
Human nature wars within me.
O, weak and miserable soul that I am!
I do what I shouldn't,
And not what I should.
Who will deliver me from this wretched body?

Praise God, for through Jesus Christ,
I am set free,
Free from the law of sin and death.
In Him, I am a new creation.
His love poured out at the cross
Covers me with the robe of righteousness.
In Him and through Him,
I have the power to become all I am meant to be.
No longer a slave to sin
But an heir of God
And co-heir with Christ.

1 Corinthians

My wisdom, my goodness, my knowledge...
All meaningless without You, O Christ.
My strength, my help, my guidance...
All futile without You, O Lord.
Without You, I am nothing, I gain nothing.

No wisdom surpasses Your wisdom.
The world's intellect is foolishness in comparison.
Your power is mightier than man's power.
Our boast is in You and You alone, O God.
Man is but a fleeting breath.

With our actions, our bodies, our very lives
We honour You, O Holy God.
You have set Your guidelines before us,
That we nay not falter or waver.
You have made us a light in a world of darkness.

Love... God's trademark.
By the grace of God, I am what I am,
For, love is not without effect.
In love, I am sealed and bonded,
Without Love, I am nothing, I gain nothing.

2 Corinthians

A thorn in my flesh was given me,
A messenger of Satan tormented me.
Powerless in myself, I relied on the Lord,
For when I am weak, then I am strong,
His power is perfected in my weakness.

We, the children of God, ministers of His gospel,
Will not lose heart in hardship,
Nor will we turn from our faith in persecution.
Indeed, we glory in these things,
For in such things we are built up for His glory.

I leave you words of wisdom and sound advice:
Be authentic, not superficial.
Be of one mind and live in peace,
Aim for perfection, realizing Christ is in you,
In so doing, you glorify the Lord your God.

Galatians

Woe is the child of slavery!
He constantly reaches for freedom
But never succeeds.
Rules, laws, regulations,
How can he uphold it all?
Hopelessly, he remains a slave to the law.

Blessed is the child of faith!
Freedom, he possesses.
Not through works, but through faith,
Faith in Jesus, who sets him free,
Free from shackles of sin and guilt,
Free from eternal damnation.

Woe is the child who turns back!
Back to the law which held him captive.
O, the poor confused soul,
He has forgotten
Deeds are the result of salvation
Not the way to salvation.

Ephesians

Stand up; stand up soldiers of Christ,
For the battle rages on furiously.
The enemy charges full force
Intent to bring nothing less than destruction.

Stand up; stand up soldiers of Christ,
For the battle is not against flesh and blood
But against God's adversary
And all his dark forces.

Stand up; stand up soldiers of Christ,
Clothe yourselves with the armour of God.
Take up the shield of faith
And the sword of the Spirit.

Stand up; stand up soldiers of Christ,
Stand strong in the Name of the Lord
Then the enemy will be rendered powerless
And yours will be the victory.

Philippians

"For me, to live is Christ,
And to die is gain."

O glorious glorious day,
When I will see Him
Face to face.
My heart melts within me
At the very thought of it,
O glorious glorious day.
Yes indeed,
To die is gain.

O happy happy day,
When I reach the end of my journey
And look back in awe
To see what He accomplished
With me for His glory,
O happy happy day.
Yes truly,
To live is Christ.

"Christ will be exalted in my body,
Whether by life or by death."

Colossians

The skies are dark.

Gloom hovers over the land.

Anger, rage, malice, slander...

These form the canopy over my heart.

Hollow and deceptive philosophy fills my mind.

Dead in sin, alienated from God,

I live to the world and its wicked ways,

Eternal death is my destiny.

In the magnitude of His love,

God rolled back the clouds of death.

At the cross, He disarmed the powers of darkness;

By His blood, new life flowed through me.

He garbed me with His robe of Righteousness

And set His Spirit within me.

I rejoice in Jesus Christ, my Lord and Savior

For I was dead but now I live.

1 Thessalonians

What!

Are we to live our lives as heathens?

Are we to carry the Lord's Name dishonourably?

No way!

We are called to live a holy life,

To be sanctified and blameless before God.

What!

Will we allow hardship to weaken our faith?

And tribulation to crush us?

No way!

Our hope in the Lord inspires our endurance,

And love prompts our labor.

What!

Brothers what is the will of God?

Is it not to love the Lord wholeheartedly,

And to love one another?

Yes way!

Then, let us put on faith and love,

For in so doing, we glorify and honour God.

2 Thessalonians

O Satan, enemy of God,
How vast is your outrage!
In brutal force, you lash out in every direction.
You, who is without compassion and mercy,
You know full well your end is near.

O child of God,
Arm yourself with the full armour of God.
The enemy is out to destroy,
Out to wreak havoc here on Earth,
So precious child, stand firm, stand strong.

With the splendor of His coming
And the breath of His mouth,
Christ will overthrow and defeat the great enemy.
By His power, He will fulfill His good purpose
And with Him, we will reign in victory forevermore.

1 Timothy

Put on your armour, my son,

And fight the good fight.

Guard what has been entrusted to your care.

Don't mingle with false knowledge

For it has turned many from the faith.

Fight my son; fight the good fight of the faith.

The Kingdom of God

Which is within you

Is not built on human knowledge

But solely on faith.

Its foundation is not of concrete

But its sure foundation is Christ our Savior.

Strive to be a good minister of Christ Jesus.

Be of a sound mind and a pure conscience.

Confess the sound doctrine

And keep from senseless controversies.

Be rich in good deeds,

Pursue godliness and righteousness.

Fight my son;

Fight the good fight of the faith.

And now,

To God be honour and glory

Forever and ever

Amen!

2 Timothy

We have fought the good fight.
By the Spirit of power, love and self-discipline,
We put our mind, body and soul under control,
We have kept love from growing cold,
And we have endured hardship.

We have finished the race.
We pursued righteousness,
Ran from wickedness,
Sought after a godly life
And fulfilled our purpose.

We have kept the faith.
Our hope stood firm,
Our trust unshakable,
Our joy complete
And our hearts steadfast.

And now,
For all who long for His appearing,
We await a crown of righteousness
To be awarded on that day
By God, our Righteous Judge.

Titus

Lord You are a God of harmony and order.
You lead Your people uprightly.
Your directions are perfect and trustworthy.

You establish leaders,
To build Your holy church,
Men, holy, disciplined and self-controlled.

With great anticipation
We look forward to Your glorious return.
You are living hope for a dying world.

Philemon

At a time of confusion and emptiness,
When my soul was as low as it could go,
Christ took me in and loved me as His own.
He restored my forlorn life
And set my enslaved soul free.
He opened my eyes
And restored a flawed relationship.
He paid in full the steep price of my debt.
I am no longer a slave
But an heir with God my Father.

Hebrews

Sweet Jesus, You came down from the throne
And became a little lower than the angels.
At the cross,
You disclosed the depth of Your love and faithfulness.
You destroyed the power of sin and death.
As High Priest, You minister on our behalf.
How great Thou art, O my God!

You are the Righteous Judge, a Consuming Fire,
The Author of salvation,
The Great Shepherd,
Intercessor and Mediator
The God of grace and mercy.
Amazing grace, how precious Thou art O God!
Only a fool would demean such love.

To You O God, I lift up my soul.
I declare Your greatness amongst the people.
I sing of Your mighty works and wonders.
I hold dear to my heart the faith I profess.
And consider Your majestic love.
I approach the throne of grace with confidence.
I love You Lord, I love You .

James

Trials and temptations,
Can any good come from such things?
Yet,
Through these my faith is being built up,
And through perseverance, I mature.
How awesome are His ways!

The Lord is a compassionate and merciful God,
Mighty in power and justice.
He desires truth,
Purity of heart and a right spirit.
He calls for action in our faith,
And patience in suffering.

Come then, O His saints,
Be steadfast in the Lord.
Seek the wisdom that comes from heaven
And live a life worthy of Christ.
Glorify Him in your perseverance
Then He will be the joy of your soul.

1 Peter

Walk on, walk on dear Christian.

Walk the righteous walk.

Many are the paths that lead to ruin,

Desirous to the eye, enchanting to the mind.

Though its appearance seems valid,

T'is but a seductive illusion that leads to destruction.

Take heed, child, not to walk in death's trap.

Walk on, walk on dear Christian.

Walk the righteous walk.

There is but one path that leads to life.

Though difficult and perplexing

T'is the path that leads to eternal glory.

Walk on, walk on child,

For you do not walk it alone.

2 Peter

The word of the Lord speaks loud and clear.
It is the word of wisdom and knowledge.
It is life to my soul.
I will meditate therein day and night.
How precious is Your word O God!
Hallelujah!

Hear, O you His saints,
Hear the inspired word of God,
For the word of the Lord is open to you.
May you understand its message,
May it take root in your mind, heart and soul.
Hallelujah!

Your word, O Lord is truly wholesome.
It is living bread, daily sustenance.
Your word is a lamp revealing hope and strength.
It voices the secrets of Your heart.
Your word, O Lord speaks peace and love to me.
Hallelujah!

1 John

Come brother; let us sing the song of love,
The song our fathers sang so long ago,
The song of joy and of peace.
Sing the Father's amazing love song.

Come brother, come walk the talk.
Let us walk the walk of righteousness
And be a witness of love.
Let us carry the flame which dispels darkness.

Come children; are we to love God and not our brother?
Surely, they are inseparable.
Love and hatred do not mix
Just as oil and water do not.

Come children; let us walk the walk of love
And walk as our holy fathers did.
Let us live out our love song
And follow Love's footsteps.

2 John

Woman,
Truth adorns you and your children.
You are looked upon with delight
By all who walk in truth.
Let love be your aspiration,
Obedience your path.
Be on guard for deceivers who roam about
To delude and destroy anyone they can.
Be careful not to be duped in their deception
And hence lose all you've laboured for.
Walk in truth, walk in love, walk in Christ.

3 John

**"I have no greater joy than to hear that
my children are walking in the truth."**

O faithful child of God
Most blessed are you,
For you walk in truth
And your life mirrors that which is in your heart.
You direct many to the righteous path.

But you, O unfaithful child of God
Cursed are you,
For you are blind to your own destructive ways.
You deceive yourself
As you walk the self- righteous path.

"Dear friend, do not imitate what is evil but what is good."

Jude

March on, O soldiers of the Most High.

The Lord reigns now and forevermore.

March in His Holy Name.

Worthy is He to be exalted and honoured.

Raise your banner

And march in God's love.

Fight the good fight of the faith.

Christ is your Sovereign Lord.

March in His love and mercy.

Shed light to them who doubt,

And snatch others out of the fire.

March in God's strength and power.

Beware; the godless have slipped in beside you.

They seek their own glory, their own honour.

They walk in ignorance, oblivious to God's authority.

They follow their own evil desires, tainting their armour.

They march to the land of self-destruction,

Where they will lay waste, twice dead.

March on, O soldiers of the Most High

Follow the Captain of your souls.

He will keep you from falling,

And proudly present you worthy before God.

So march with confidence and assurance,

March on to great victory.

Revelation

The Lord Faithful and True,

Will avenge the blood of His saints.

The devil, the great deceiver

Will be hurled into the lake of burning sulfur

Along with the beast and the false prophet.

They will be tormented day and night forevermore.

They whose name is not found written in the book of life

Will be thrown in the lake of fire which is the second death.

Rejoice, you Saints of God!

Rejoice and be glad,

The wedding of the Lamb has come,

And His bride has made herself ready.

She is beautifully dressed for her husband,

Clothed in fine linen, bright and clean.

Rejoice and be glad.

Again, I say rejoice!

The New Jerusalem, O Holy City,

Bride of the Lamb,

You shine in the glory of God.

Your brilliance is like a precious jewel, clear as crystal.

Nothing impure, nor anyone false-hearted

Will enter within Your gates,

Only they whose name is written in the book of life.
Blessed are they who are invited to the wedding supper.

King of kings and Lord of lords,
The Alpha and the Omega,
The Beginning and the End,
The Root and the Offspring of David,
The Bright Morning Star,
We long for You.
The Bridegroom says, "I am coming soon."
Amen! Come Lord Jesus, come.

Invitation

There is a myth that there is a fountain of youth somewhere in this world that promises eternal youth to all who drink of its water. Some people actually believe it exists.

Although the majority of us know this fountain of youth is nothing but a fallacy, there is a Fountain of great worth that truly exists. It is one that promises eternal life to all who drink of its water. The Fountain is found in the Lord and Saviour Jesus Christ... "Whoever drinks the water I give him will never thirst. Indeed, the water I give him will become in him a spring of water welling up to eternal life." (John 4:14)

No one will ever be turned away who comes to Jesus. "Come! Whoever is thirsty, let him come; and whoever wishes, let him take the free gift of the water of life." (Revelations 22:17)

The way to the Fountain of Eternal life is as simple as ABC...
   A) **Admit** you are a sinner and repent of your sins. For all have sinned and fall short of the glory of God." (Romans 3:23)
   B) **Believe** you have eternal life though Jesus Christ who died for you. Call on Him. "For God so loved the world that he gave his one and only Son, that whoever believes in Him shall not perish but have eternal life. (John 3:16)
   C) **Commit** your life to Jesus Christ, to live for Him and serve Him. "So then, those who suffer according to God's will should commit themselves to their faithful Creator and continue to do good." (1 Peter 4:19)

Jesus is the only way, the whole truth and the life eternal. Choose you this day whom you will serve. Please my friend, choose wisely and do not delay for your future depends on it.

In Christ,

Paulyne Cascanette

CPSIA information can be obtained at www.ICGtesting.com
Printed in the USA
LVOW08*0932130913

352210LV00004B/6/P